Bygones presented by Anglia T

ANTIQUES AND

Twenty years in my shop

Prynne Hutton

The Boydell Press · Ipswich

Published by The Boydell Press Ltd
PO Box 24 Ipswich IP1 1JJ

ISBN 0 85115 091 8

Printed in Great Britain by
Lowe & Brydone Printers Limited, Thetford, Norfolk

Foreword

Following the first set of BYGONES booklets published in 1976 several people sent me manuscripts they had written. I read them all and wished that we could publish more than just a few.

Having written it, Prynne Hutton seemed concerned that her story wouldn't interest many people. Having read it, I think differently because I am sure amongst the vast audience of television viewers who watch BYGONES there must be a great number of people who are interested in antiques, bric-a-brac, knick-knacks and all the paraphernalia that is found in small antique shops in towns and villages throughout the country.

The story tells how she got started with her shop, where she went to find the objects to sell, how she coped with customers and all the other day to day problems that go with transferring any item from one family household to another through the dealer. Her story of the little shop in a quiet Suffolk village surrounded by the colourful character of her customers, dealers, honest men and rogues, and the vivid descriptions of houses, auction rooms and farms makes, to my mind, delightful reading for anyone interested in a way of life outside the "concrete jungle".

Dick Joice

DICK JOICE

Beginnings

People always ask, "Why did you start an antique shop?" "When did you start one?" "What put the idea into your head?" "How did you begin?"

I think the answer is rather the same as "Why did you start a love affair?" – because it was compelling, and almost unavoidable. But as with a love affair or marriage, what is comparatively easy to begin with needs a lot of thought, work and constant attention if it is to be successful. These qualities grow with experience if you can stick things out, as also do the enjoyment and pleasure.

I was about to say that it was a great deal easier to start twenty years ago, when I did, than it is today. But on considering that statement I think perhaps it is wrong, and that it is in fact easier to start today, but less rewarding and adventurous. It is easier because there is much more technical knowledge available on all sides, and often more ready money at hand for the would-be beginner. It is also possible to start nowadays with a stall in an antique market, or if your stock is mixed and unorthodox with a stall one day a week in an ordinary market town, so that if you have not much to sell you can spread your wares out to look interesting, while you keep your ears and eyes open and learn the trade gradually before you go to the expense of renting a shop.

A seaside resort or tourist centre, with its ever-changing public, can be an excellent place for a beginner who is tough enough and thick-skinned enough to brazen out his mistakes, and ignore the comments of other more hard-bitten dealers.

I myself began in a very small way indeed, just twenty years ago. My capital was about £30 and I had a cupboard full of oddments that had been bargains, but had really no place in the small house where my husband and I lived.

I was at a loose end and already nearing middle age and, because of a bout of ill-health, had had to give up rearing Jersey heifers, which had been my absorbing occupation until that time. I was very interested in old things and I liked talking to people. And let me say at once that to make a success of a small shop these two characteristics are almost essential – that is, unless one has a huge knowledge of some specific type of antique, be it pottery, porcelain or what have you, which I did not have when I started my shop.

Oddly enough, there are a good many dealers whose heads are crammed with invaluable knowledge, who have an intense feeling of irritation towards the less well-informed public – and are inclined to say tersely behind the customers back "He wouldn't know a T'Ang Dynasty vase from a modern ginger jar out of the next door grocers", when speaking of a would-be customer. But how, I wonder, can a new collector be expected to know so much? He has very likely never brought his mind round to such things before, has never handled them. He is only now, through some chance awakening of interest, wanting to learn.

Occasionally one comes across the very erudite dealer who is longing to impart his technical information to anyone who shows the slightest glimmer of interest, but sadly he often holds forth too long upon his pet subject, and the customer goes away with his head reeling with dates and obscure information that in all probability he is never going to need.

My knowledge of the things I sell has come very slowly and often painfully, and is still filtering through in a slightly incoherent mass of unrelated facts, but my interest in people has always been enormous. So in all probability you will find I give more anecdotes in my book than hard facts about the business, although I hope there will be some of those as well, that can be of help to a beginner in "The Trade".

Anyhow, I can boast in all honesty that from a tiny shop in a remote Suffolk village, I have built up a business known to hundreds of private customers and many dealers as well.

But please don't run away with the idea that keeping an antique shop is an easy way of life. It isn't – unless you have a great deal of capital behind you, and the knowledge that it doesn't really matter if you succeed or not.

When I started my shop I lived in a world of grey and crumpled newspaper, seas of it, mounting ceiling-wards, often stained and smelly, blackening my hands and nails. For this is what we use for packing. Occasionally I had nightmares when I knew that somewhere amongst that drifting mass of paper was a tiny piece of rare china I had failed to remember when I unpacked the heavy old jugs, the chipped blue and white plates, so slight and small it was, so delicate; and at any moment some kind, misguided friend or customer would come into the office crying breezily, "I'll clear this stuff up for you", and I would wake sweating to the sound of snapping, crunching china beneath my kind friend's enormous feet.

It does happen. Something small and rather precious is left in the bottom of the box unnoticed, just because it has been packed so carefully in crumpled paper. Dealers' boxes and cartons are used over and over again, and sometimes not unpacked for two or three days. I can remember suffering a sad blow once, over which I was forced to smile politely, when a regular, pleasant but slightly woolly-minded customer phoned me to say, "It was so sweet of you to put in the surprise for me."

"Oh yes," I murmured vaguely.

"I only found it when I had unpacked the teaset, right at the bottom of the box."

"I am awfully glad you are pleased," I said, while my mind groped to discover what she was talking about. Her next words – "I so love the puppy's expression as it looks up at its sedate mother" – brought hateful and precise understanding, and I knew I must have left a small porcelain group of a poodle and her pup, in the bottom of the box.

I had meant to keep it for my own collection. It was charming, and far more valuable than my woolly friend would ever realise. But what could I do? I cut her string of thanks short, and I hope my voice was still pleasant as I remarked, "I really must go – there is someone in the shop. I am glad that you are pleased." After all, I suppose it was as well somebody was.

I was, I am sure, very lucky in the way in which my own business got started.

Soon after we had moved into the village, I became very intrigued by a tiny lock-up shop two doors away from our house, and almost opposite the village green. There were about five or six pottery bowls in the window, and nothing else. The prices were clearly marked on the bowls, and a small notice said, "Apply to the cottage opposite". This was the home of the former village baker and his wife, Mr and Mrs Gowing, who at one period had lived in the house that was now ours, and I had talked to them about our garden and the lovely lilac tree they had planted years ago, and the old pump, and the pony stable at the end of the long garden path, so I knew them quite well.

"I'd like to buy one of the little blue pots out of the shop," I said, and Mr Gowing, a tall, good-looking old man, heaved himself out of his Windsor chair before the fire, reached for a key hanging on a beam, and came across the road with me.

"They are made by an artist lady who comes here weekends," he explained, as he fitted the key into the lock. The door opened in two halves like a stable one, I noticed, and the small room we entered was really part of a large cottage, but was now sealed off from the main building.

"Used to sell nails and hinges and door latches and such, years ago," Mr Gowing told me, and pointed to the rows and rows of small drawers behind the old elm counter.

To me it was an enchanting little shop with its wide counter, the bow window with two shelves for display, and an old well-worn brick floor. There was also a round topped, coloured glass door that had once led into the ironmonger's parlour, but was now blocked up on the other side.

I bought the pottery soup bowl and learned more about the person who made them. "She's got that little cottage on the side near the green," Mr Gowing explained. "I reckon she don't come down more than six or seven times a year. She's always off to foreign parts and such. But then, she's an artist, and you know what they are." His grey eyes twinkled, and he added, "As nice a lady as they come, but as helter-skelter as a box full of mice."

"Does she sell much?"

"No," he told me, "and as likely as not if I get her an order for a dozen soup bowls all to match, she just don't feel like making that sort no more, so that's the end of it. It can't pay her rent."

That night I thought about the little shop a great deal. It took me right back to two books I had loved as a child: "A Flat Iron for a Farthing" by Mrs Ewing, about a small boy who had stayed in a saddler's shop; but better still to me was one called "Maidie's Little Shop". It was, as far as I can remember, a very pious Victorian story about an eight year old child with a bedridden mother, who to help the family fortunes had turned the front room of the cottage into a little sweet shop. It had all been an enormous success, of course, and in the end even the lady of the manor bought lollipops from Maidie, and Mamma took to her feet again.

But it was not the hint of bravery and high endeavour in the story that appealed to me. It was the description of things like the scrubbed counter, the brass weighing machine, the window full of glass jars, and the taking of pennies and halfpennies into the small wooden bowl in the counter drawer, that completely enthralled me. My grandmother, who died before I was born, owned a shop in a small Cornish town, so maybe I had inherited the longing to own one from her.

A few weeks later, the artist who made the little bowls came down to stay at her cottage, and without giving myself much time to think I approached her and asked if she would consider sharing the shop with me.

"What do you want to sell – are you a potter too?" she asked. "No," I explained, "I'd just like to sell odds and ends and try to make the window look pretty – perhaps sell flowers and eggs and fruit as well – I really don't quite know myself. But of course I would put your pottery in the centre of the window."

Instantly she too was fired with enthusiasm. "And I will make patchwork quilts and cushions, and plates with children's names on them."

"We will share the rent," I suggested.

"It's awfully low" – she mentioned a figure, and indeed it was incredibly low – "but really," she went on, in her vague and charming way, "you needn't pay any of it, as you will be doing all the selling."

But I insisted on paying half, and when I consider how soon and how completely I took over that little shop, I am ashamed I did not pay the whole rent from the very beginning.

But I did not know Dorothy as well in those days as I do now. An artist to her finger tips, feckless, unreliable and enormously kind-hearted.

One patchwork quilt appeared and was duly sold, perhaps a dozen more pieces of pottery, a charming little painting of a small child with a rabbit, and then nothing. Dorothy had taken to oil painting and mosaics in a big way – she just could not give her mind to selling or preparing anything for sale.

Meanwhile, I had collected all the unwanted oddments from my cupboard and had mounted old prints and put them into discarded frames and arranged them round the shop. I marked everything in very plain figures, and I had a tray outside on which each item was marked either 3d or 6d. I also made a point of saying on the label if anything was cracked or damaged. And then, feeling rather like a spider at the centre of its web, I sat and waited.

At least my stock was very mixed. It varied from Staffordshire figures to iron frying pans, huge flat cream dishes from my dairy, rolls of stair carpet and children's toys.

Within a fortnight I had almost sold out. The people from the village came almost every day, for it was such a novelty to have a junk shop in their midst.

There was a big, good-natured Cockney woman who never failed to "pop in" on her way back from her cleaning job, to see if there was anything suitable for "our Pam" or "our Maureen", or even something for the dog, like a big drinking bowl, or an old sharp knife to cut up his food. She adored giving presents.

Now, after twenty years, she still pops in, but more for a gossip these days. "You've gone all posh now, dear," she says accusingly.

Sales

I soon realised that if I was to carry on with an adequately stocked shop, I should have to go to sales, or try to buy privately. There was a bus from our village to Colchester, the nearest big town, where two sales each week were held, with the view days on Mondays and Tuesdays. Plucking up my courage but slightly daunted by the memory of the large and alarming cattle sales I had attended at Reading, I arrived early at the sale room and installed myself in a seat in the back row of chairs arranged round the rostrum. My head was buzzing with stories I had been told, of how a raised eyebrow, a fluttered catalogue, could land you with a lot like a stuffed bear or an electric cooker that would never work again. So I sat hunched and immobile during that first sale, poring over my catalogue, and assiduously marking the prices paid for each lot.

Some of these astounded me, and I wished – too late – that I had had the courage to bid. A charming little black and gilt bracket and an enormous overmantel with a broken mirror glass, went for five shillings. I could have sold the bracket, I knew, for a pound or more, at the drop of a hat. It was only later that it dawned on me that I should have had to remove the repellent, two hundredweight overmantel by next morning, not later than twelve o'clock. Nor was it the sort of thing that would have been accepted as a gift, by the strange hangers-on who always attend sales, awaiting the free armchair, or this and that (which just will not fit on the dealer's roof rack and isn't worth a second journey), or the set of good aluminium saucepans that someone has been forced to buy to get a Georgian copper kettle.

At that first sale I bought nothing, but at my second I had the temerity to spend £5 and acquire seven lots. I had no car then, but in those days our village carrier was perfectly willing, not only to collect from the saleroom, but to pack the various lots into cartons and tea chests, and deliver them that night or the next morning. Moreover, in all the years he worked for me he never smashed a thing. Dear Harold Andrews – I miss him still.

When my purchases arrived my excitement knew no bounds. Those were the days when a tin bath full of china and oddments were lumped together in one lot, and often the auctioneer himself hardly knew what they contained.

My seven lots covered the whole of the sitting room floor when they were unpacked, and we looked at them in amazement and excitement – and in my husband's case, I think with faint horror as well. For amongst the jumble of desirable objects that I had thought worth bidding for, were chipped pie dishes, a broken mincing machine, a chamber pot with no handle and revolting yellow stains. But there was a brass candlestick, a Sheffield plate wine strainer, a cuckoo clock, and a completely new set of glasses still wrapped up in tissue paper, not to mention a number of charming shopping baskets, some table mats and a very large, slightly chipped Staffordshire dog.

Within a week I had sold everything that hadn't to go straight into the dustbin, and made what seemed to me a fair profit.

"It seems so extraordinary, almost immoral," I said to my husband, "because any woman in the village could have got on a bus and gone to that saleroom and bought the things for what I gave. Why should I get all that extra on them?"

I was at that time very green indeed. Also, my husband was still in a job. But the time was coming very soon when his work was going to end, and our small shop would have to become our mainstay. It is possible that because at the back of my mind I realised this as the months went by, that I put all my energy into making the business a success, continually planning how I could expand my trade, and learning all I could from other dealers. And there were many who were kind enough to help me with my various problems, giving me sound, if rather alarming advice.

Betsy

It was at the end of my first few months' trading that I met Betsy. I already knew her by sight, and had learned that she lived in a charming small Georgian house in a nearby village.

I saw her first from a pub window one Sunday morning. She and her husband were walking home from church, or perhaps I should say they were promenading along the main street of her village, stopping to admire a new baby, or have a few words with old Mr Sadler, who cut the grass round the tombstones. We were still rather new to that part of Suffolk, and apart from the landlord of the Horse Shoes, knew few people in this particular village, which was almost four miles from where we lived.

"I should think they must be the people from the Manor," I said to my husband, and watched them with appreciation, for they were both well worth attention.

She was a beautiful middle-aged woman, wearing an impeccable tweed suit, a charming and obviously very expensive hat. Her shoes and handbag were of crocodile skin, and the gloves she carried so negligently were of the finest hand-stitched leather. Her husband, a great deal older – in fact, almost an old man – was spare and straight, and his pepper and salt tweeds, although not new, were splendidly tailored.

When they turned again at the end of the street, and once more passed the window, I asked the girl behind the bar who they were.

"Oh, that's Mrs Kay and the Colonel, live in the old red house on the hill. She's mad about sales, goes to every one for miles around, and if you want anything like a bed or a table or a dinner service, you've only got to ask her, and like as not she'll get it in a week or so."

This in itself seemed an extraordinary statement, for at first sight I would have thought business, specially the second-hand sort, would be the very last thing in which so elegant a person would dabble.

But indeed the next time I saw Betsy was at a small, rather scruffy farm sale, where all the first lots were piled against the barn side in old tin trunks or pig troughs. To my amazement, she was leaning over one of these receptacles, checking carefully through the contents, which seemed to me to consist of battered photo frames, old calendars, jars of pickles; probably everything from a dresser drawer that had been shot into it, to get rid of the stuff somehow.

She was still wearing good tweeds and shoes, but her well arranged grey hair was uncovered, and her hands were grimy. At her heels trotted a couple of white, rather wooden looking bull terriers. The Colonel, meanwhile, sat in the car, alternately dozing in the golden autumn sunshine and glancing at The Times.

So I too started to ferret among the unsavoury looking heaps, convinced that if they were worth Betsy's attention, they would most certainly be worth mine. But, alas, I could see nothing worth a shilling bid – but I was, I admit, put off by the smell and the squalid jumble of useless objects.

She stood watching me for a minute or two, and then she smiled and said, "Nothing much there today, but you never know." To my amazement her voice was broad Suffolk, nor did she make the least attempt to feign a purer accent than the one that came naturally to her. She then said, "Let me introduce you to my darlings," and she called "Jess, Sukey," and the pink-faced bull terriers came bounding up, banging at me with their hard heads, all loving enthusiasm. "Bad Sukey, bad Jess," Betsy cooed, and she sounded like an adoring mother with obstreperous children.

During that sale at the little farm I watched Betsy, for she fascinated me, and there was nothing much I wanted to bid for myself. To my amazement she bought over twenty lots, including a bath full of seeming rubbish, and almost anything else that went for a few shillings.

I, meanwhile, had rather foolishly bought a large chest of drawers, and had had to find a friend with a van to help me collect it. In the late afternoon, when we came back for it, nearly everyone had disappeared with their bargains, but Betsy and the Colonel were still loading up their old-fashioned car. It was bulging with strange objects, almost like a rag and bone merchant's cart.

"This is our third load," she called gaily to me. "Lots of rubbish, but saleable, and look at these." She opened her handbag and took out a beautiful miniature on ivory, in its original frame. It was of a young girl in a high-waisted Regency dress and a yellow turban. It was spattered with what appeared to be blackcurrant jam or beetroot pickle, but that was only on the glass. The second object was a tiny pinchbeck box in the shape of an acorn, beautifully fashioned and I should think unique.

"But I didn't see them," I gasped in envy.

"At the bottom of the tin trunk," she laughed. "I hid them up again in all those old jars and calendars. I got the whole lot for five shillings."

I had no words, but at least Betsy had taught me one lesson, that it is well to learn early in this trade, not to be finicky and ladylike.

"I'll probably see you at the next sale," she called as they drove away. And indeed I did, and the next, and the next. But actually I saw her even before that, and in the following years we became both good friends and good enemies.

A few weeks later she phoned to say she had got lots of "darling treasures" to show me, and could she come and fetch me that very afternoon. I was, as usual in those days, getting short of stock, so I accepted her offer very gratefully. To say that I was bewildered by that first visit was to put it mildly. Her own sitting and dining rooms were immaculate, full of charmingly arranged flowers. There was a wide open fireplace with blazing logs, and a low table set out with tea things on a lace cloth.

"First we will have tea," she said, "and then I'll show you all my treasure in the stable."

But even as we drank our tea, poured from a magnificent Georgian teapot, she was darting about the room, opening drawers and offering me small pieces of jewellery, snuff boxes and lengths of old lace. When we had finished she led me out to the stables. "We must be careful how we open the doors, or everything may fall on top of us," she told me, laughing.

I thought she was speaking figuratively, but indeed she was not; as the door swung back there was a crash and we were enveloped in a pile of screens, cushions, towel horses, small brackets and pictures. Books of every sort lay piled on the floor, many rotting already in the damp, while the stable and coach house behind were stacked nearly to the roof with furniture of all sorts, mostly in need of repair of some kind. It was enthralling, and many of the objects were much greater bargains than I had the knowledge to realise at that time.

Betsy was a wonderful saleswoman. She managed to imbue everything she wanted to sell with a kind of glamour, and it was only very slowly that I learned to beware of what my husband termed "Betsy's darlings".

But she was good fun, with an enormous zest for life, and over the years I did get some wonderful bargains from her, but only, I am afraid, after I had learned to meet guile with guile.

On that first visit, after we had raked through the stable and coach house, and even the old outside earth closet, Betsy led me into the house again and up the stairs.

"This is really my spare room," she explained, and opened the door into a charming room in the wildest disorder, the bed, the chest of drawers, the floor strewn with objects, many of which still bore their lot numbers.

By this time my head was in a whirl and I wasn't really sure what I had bought, although Betsy was busy making out a list with a stub of pencil, on a torn envelope. It was already nearly seven o'clock and I was wanting to get home to put a pie in the oven and stew some apples for our evening meal. But as Betsy was ferrying me to and fro, it was difficult to demand that she took me home.

Out meal was very late that night, but I had learned another lesson, which was – unless I had a lot of time to spare, I must not accept an invitation to be "fetched".

I became rather exasperated when Betsy dragged God into her transactions, which she often did, and with real sincerity, I think, for she was a very religious person, with the simple faith of a child. She was, for instance, quite convinced that she wore her madly expensive hats to church to the glory of God, and she could not understand why I once accused her of talking nonsense when she said she could not afford to buy grilling steak for the Colonel, although a day or so before she had spent eight guineas on a hat, and fourteen on a handbag.

"But he loves me to have pretty things. Nothing makes him happier. A man likes to be proud of his woman, and see her well turned out."

I think now, maybe she really spoke the truth, for he was inordinately proud of her; but at that time I often thought how thin and frail he looked, and wondered if he should have been allowed to lug such heavy furniture and boxes about, without at least the reward of a good steak occasionally. But then, I know I have got a very material mind.

Betsy couldn't on the whole be bothered with cooking, which was odd when you think she came of East Anglian farming stock. But she made her house beautiful with antique furniture and lovely brocades, and her garden was charming. When the mood took her she would work in it for days on end, altering brick paths, cutting vistas through thick hedges, and struggling with huge stones to make a rockery. But every alteration had to be shown to, and admired by whoever she could entice within her orbit. I have never known a woman who needed so much praise. And she could take flattery, even of the most blatant sort, by the bucketful.

There were auctioneers and other dealers who traded on this childish vanity, but I am afraid I often found it exhausting in the extreme, and after some time with her tended to grow sour and waspish – inwardly, at least. Yet I often think of a rather endearing idea she once expounded to me. She was showing me some ornaments of her own that were on the top shelf of her dresser. As she turned them over in her hands the dust flew off in a little cloud. "Oh dear, I haven't looked at them with my glasses on for ages – I didn't know they were so dirty," she exclaimed.

"I'm sure all mine on the top shelves are just the same," I told her, "because I don't see things like that either, if I haven't my specs on."

"Yes. You know, I'm sure that's the reason we can't see so well."

I looked puzzled. "I mean," she said very earnestly, "I think God arranges it like that, so we don't see all the dirt when we get older, because we can't do so much cleaning, and as we can't see it, it doesn't worry us."

"Well, maybe you're right," I agreed, "but all the same, I'd be glad if I didn't need glasses."

"But aren't they a clever invention," she enthused. "It's so wonderful of God."

"Yes," I said, "Yes, indeed."

Brass Tacks

But I must get down to brass tacks, and the really practical things one has to learn as the owner of an antique-cum-junk shop. I think one of the most important things, to begin with, is not to set one's sights too high. In fact, be willing to buy saleable rubbish on occasion, just to keep things moving while learning from experience and from the kindness of other dealers.

Certainly, quite a lot can be learned from books, especially well illustrated ones, but the trouble with most books is that they are dealing with the sort of objects that seldom come within the range of a small shopkeeper who is just starting. They help, I think, to educate your eye for that chance in a hundred when something rare does turn up, and also may make you set yourself a sort of yardstick by which to judge shapes and the prevalence of certain types of decoration that often appear at given periods over and over again, and follow through at those dates from the most expensive objects to the cottager's imitation of grandeur. So by all means study books on antiques, when you have the time. But to my way of thinking, handling an object teaches you a great deal more than any amount of reading will do. This is where I found that for the first two years the endless attending of sales proved my best education.

On the view day I would carefully examine lots and note in my catalogue the price I expected an article to fetch, in auction. Not things I meant to bid for, but those which I admired, or thought I would like to possess, or even those I just considered valuable. On the day of the sale I attended again with my pencilled catalogue, and jotted down in red ink the actual price the lot fetched, alongside my guessed one. I was often appalled at the difference. I had usually made very bad mistakes both ways, occasionally valuing something too high, but more often incredibly low compared with the price it reached.

As the months went by I learned the names of the various dealers who attended the salerooms. Many of them were friendly people, so that after a while, when I had made some ridiculously low guess, I plucked up the courage to ask them about the things they had bought.

One man in particular was very kind, and took time and trouble to show me the porcelain he had purchased.

"It's early Worcester," he told me, as he lifted a cup and saucer, and put them carefully into my hands, "and that little bowl is New Hall, and the sparrow-beaked jug is Lowestoft."

"But how on earth do you know? They none of them have marks."

"Feel them," he told me, "hold them up to the light. Worcester paste has that greeny tinge, while Lowestoft is soft paste and the glaze often has a blue look, and as a rule it runs over the bottoms of mugs and jugs, covering the rims. Leeds ware has a very distinctive light, smooth feel – you'd soon learn to recognise Leeds."

I had learned by this time to hold small objects very carefully, with both hands if possible, even if it meant dumping my precious handbag on the floor of the saleroom.

The dealer smiled at my bewildered concentration.

"Come along to my shop and I will show you some good porcelain, and I expect my wife will show you her collection of Staffordshire figures."

"It's terribly kind of you and I'd love to come, but I sometimes feel I'll never learn. I am awfully bad at names and dates and that sort of thing – in fact I have never passed an examination in my life."

But in spite of myself, I was about to write, I was very gradually learning; I have not, however, even after all this time, become good at remembering the names of factories and porcelain painters. But what I have learned about is quality and period. I cannot often say with complete confidence "This is Coalport, Worcester, Derby," but I can say "This is eighteenth century and is a good example of its sort," or even when it is ugly or grotesque, I can feel pretty sure it was made before the year 1800, or else that it is about 1850 or 1870, or whatever; and to have learned that is an enormous help when it comes to valueing and buying stock.

Almost anything you acquire, be it pottery, porcelain or bric-a-brac, that something tells you is good, but you have no understanding of *why* you think so, is best put away safely until someone you judge to be an expert in that particular type of object comes into your shop. You have to trust him, for it is often a temptation to a dealer to decry your find, in the hope of buying it cheaply.

This type of buyer will say something like "Very pretty – in a way looks almost like Chelsea, but of course it's not, it's a poor German imitation. But I'll take it off you if you like, as I've got someone who collects this sort of stuff." And he then offers a low price.

But that kind of dealer was, I am glad to say, pretty rare, anyhow in my early days, and most collectors and many dealers are willing to advise you, especially if you in your turn will try to find them the sort of things they are looking for. If, however, you are just out to pick their brains about something you are really not sure you wish to sell, it is only fair to state this fact quite clearly before you produce the object for their inspection. In most cases they are sufficiently interested to examine what you have, give an honest opinion as to what it is, and how much you could expect to get for it. If later you wish to sell it and the price they have quoted will give you a profit, you should let them have first refusal.

Many dealers have been very good to me, but maybe I have just been lucky. I can remember on one occasion I had put a small, greyish-green bowl on my cheap shelf in the shop, pricing it at about two shillings, I think, when a man who owns a shop in a town some miles away picked it up and grinned at me quizzically, "What do you think it is?" he asked. "I don't know," I told him, "but I imagined it to be something made in a pottery class that didn't turn out very well." He put it down carefully on the counter. He said, "As you know, I sell mainly furniture, and certainly not old Chinese pottery." He peeled off my sticky label with its two shilling mark, and tore it into little pieces. "But I got it for almost nothing in a lot of old rubbish at a sale," I assured him. "It doesn't matter where you got it, but have another think about it and label it £10, and I wouldn't mind betting you won't have it in your shop for more than a week or two."

He was quite right. A bent old gentleman in a chauffeur driven car snatched it up and pushed two notes across the counter. "Here is my phone number – give me a ring if you get anything else of this period." He was gone without waiting to have his purchase wrapped, and before I could discover what period it was or anything about it.

When my dealer friend next came in I recounted what had happened in great jubilation, and offered to share the £10 with him. He wouldn't take anything. "Nonsense, I am glad I was right – maybe I should have told you to mark it £20."

But I was very content not only with my lovely fat profit, but with the knowledge that something quite good had not gone to a lady seeking a cheap bowl in which to plant her Christmas bulbs, and that in that particular dealer I had found someone I would always trust. But I could not have complained if someone else had come into my shop and borne off the little bowl in triumph, for two shillings. I had made my profit, and if through greater knowledge and experience someone had gained by my mistake – well, that's all part of the game, really.

In this job one just has to have a lucky break sometimes – in other words, buy something cheaply – or we would never make a profit and cover the horrid mistakes that even the most experienced dealer makes on occasions, and it happens to all of us. Often there are times when you are tired and your "eye is out", or the light in some cottage is very poor, and when you unpack the next day in the cold light of reason in your own office, you realise you have been sold, or have bought, a pup, often quite unintentionally by the vendor of the object. In fact, you yourself may have named the price for the offending article, but no dealer of any worth will try to go back on his bad bargain – not unless he realises he has been deliberately hood-winked; and usually not then, for he knows himself to be a fool for being taken in. The best thing you can do is to sell the object at a loss, for what in fact you really believe to be its right price, or do what we all feel is legitimate, "Bung it back in a sale" and hope some other fool will make the same mistake that you did.

One dealer I know says that when he has paid too much for anything he sells it quickly at a loss to get it out of his sight, and then puts an extra 50p on to everything else he sells until he has reimbursed himself. An ingenious idea, but a little hard on the buying public, I think.

Choosing Stock

As you gain experience it is fairly safe to say your mistakes get less and less. You have not only found out what is a realistic price to pay, but you have also learned what type of buyer your shop attracts. The actual kind of building from which you operate does seem to dictate, in some way, the sort of stock you are most likely to succeed with. For instance, my shop happens to be in a very ancient Suffolk village. It has a small, old-fashioned bow window right on to the street, a simple, brick-floored place with heavy beams. Then there is a gateway that leads to a large barn with flowers growing untidily about its door, and windows looking on to trees and an orchard. Not at all the kind of shop from which to sell grand, inlaid furniture and delicate ornamental bric-a-brac.

Therefore, as time went on I found my stock tended to be mostly of the fairly inexpensive stripped pine and oak, cottage-type of furniture, bright pottery jugs and bowls, Staffordshire figures, combined with the oddly charming piece of extravagantly decorated Victorian nonsense that could be picked up cheaply in those days, and which tended to complement the plainer things. To begin with, a great many of my customers were young married couples with a sharp eye for both utility and amusement in their household schemes. They realised how well a wildly curly sofa would give quality to a severe pine dresser; that the plainest iron bedstead was enhanced by a tasselled, ornate Victorian cover; and that a very ordinary round table often looks far better when surmounted by a red glass oil lamp with a flowery china shade.

Wide gilt picture frames were in great demand to be turned into mirrors, as were the rich, glowing maple-wood ones. I think that the young to whom I mostly sold at that time loved contrasts, as in fact I do myself, so that gradually my shop was gaining a sort of character of its own. I don't mean that all I bought and sold were things I liked – I was far from being able to reach that happy standard, and about half my income has always been acquired, I suppose, by just buying bargains when I saw them, and selling them quickly at a very small profit.

"Of course, I never buy anything for my shop unless I like it myself." So speak the women whose husbands are rich, and who are running a little "boutique" for the fun of the thing. One of them once said to me, very smugly, "I would have to feel sure they are things I would put in my own home."

I am afraid when people talk like that I want to shout at them "Who the hell are you to put up your personal taste as the criterion of all that should be accepted by your customers?"

All right, discard those things you feel are really badly made, or are so distasteful to you that they make you ashamed, but as to only selling the objects one would want in one's own home, take a second thought and ask yourself, "Is my taste so impeccable that I must dictate to all those I consider not blessed with the sublime discrimination vouchsafed to me?"

The arrangement of objects, however, is a very personal thing, and the juxtaposition of certain things can alter one's outlook on them completely. In fact, I have learned, in arranging my showroom, that a display of quite mediocre blue and white plates on a dresser will sell the piece of furniture, while a couple of good decanters will do the same for a side table that has been ignored for months when it was only holding a clutter of cheap glasses.

Practicalities

I soon learned, to my discomfort at first, that it is essential to keep books. It is, of course, necessary to do so for income tax purposes, but I am not just referring to those, which friends tell me can be kept quite efficiently by means of cheque book stubs and invoices. As I am very bad indeed at figures of any sort, mine are kept in what most people would consider a very primitive way. First of all, everything I buy is written down and given a number. It is essential that you do this almost at once, because however sure you feel that you will remember exactly where you bought a thing, and what you gave for it, the chances are that even in a couple of weeks you will be unsure, especially if you are pressed for a price by someone in a hurry. I buy plain lined books, not cash books, and rule in the columns I need – first a narrow margin on the left, for the number and date. Then a wide space, with room for a fairly detailed description of the article, if it is a piece of furniture, or an outstanding bit of china or pottery, with a note of any damage I may know it has. If I buy a "lot" with a number of things in it, it is just described as "20 pieces of glass", or what have you, all given the same number. Next comes a column left blank until the article is sold. After that come two more in which is stated what I paid, not forgetting to add on transport or repair costs. Beyond come two more ruled spaces in which I put down what I get for any thing, and then the actual profit is stated, so that it can be seen at a glance. By keeping a book of this sort you can see at once how much you can reduce a given piece to other members of the trade, and also from where you are buying most profitably.

I also keep a book with the names and addresses of my regular customers, often with a small personal note of what they are most interested in, or perhaps just saying they are charming people. If they have small children I often jot down their names as well. There are also more sinister remarks in my address book, such as "Bad payers", "Beater downers", or "Have bad-mannered small boys". But those are few and far between, and a note that says "Nice, pregnant wife, husband with gorgeous red hair, both like simple oak furniture" brings back instantly memories of a charming young couple who also buy white and gold patterned china and sporting prints, as presents for each other. Customers like to be remembered, and also it is useful to be able to show them the sort of things you know they like, or even occasionally to hide away pieces that are "just them" until they next come into the shop. Here and there are other revealing notes, such as "loves dogs", "hates Mrs G H", or simply "likely to bring things back after some weeks."

Admittedly there are days when you dislike nearly all your customers. As one dealer said to me, "Wouldn't this be a lovely job if only there weren't people coming into the shop." I am afraid we all tend to dislike those people who rather gushingly describe themselves as "browsers" – not all of them, of course, with some it is just meant as a friendly warning that they may not want to buy, and they hope they are not wasting your time. To those I say at once that I know that it is very much a matter of luck, finding things in a junk shop, and I shall quite understand if they do not purchase anything.

Unless they seem to want to talk I leave them to their own devices, and busy myself with some job in the office. There are, however, some customers known to all dealers, who always manage to discover an object that has not got a price ticket. I try to have everything plainly marked, but inevitably some things lose their price tags, or newly arrived stock has come in and I have been too busy to mark it for an hour or two. I can never decide whether the person enquiring about these unticketed goods is the sort of optimist who always thinks the unmarked things are free, or that perhaps I will make a mistake in their favour.

There is one lady in particular who has a positive genius for finding unpriced articles, so much so that I have sometimes wondered if she removed labels herself. At any rate, when I see her car pull up now, I scuttle round quickly to be sure that I haven't slipped up.

I am quite sure the policy of labelling everything in plain figures is a good one, for I know how daunting it can become to some people when it is necessary to enquire the price of everything. After three or four enquiries, where the price has proved too high, they feel too abashed to go on asking, and thus may lose the very bargain that every antique shop is supposed to contain.

But easily removed sticky labels can be a snare, especially if someone else looks after your showroom for you on occasions. An elderly helper of ours was once very badly cheated. A man she did not know picked up a small figure of a Cupid and said, "This seems quite cheap – I'll take it," and he pointed to the price tag stuck on it which said 5/-. Mrs S also thought it seemed very cheap, but imagined it was made of some base metal, so she took his money, and he drove off. The figure was bronze. We found its right label of £6 hidden in a cheap vase, from which the man had peeled off the price and neatly transferred it to the Cupid. There was nothing to be done – it was just one of those things. I did try for a while putting two tags on everything, but nothing quite like that happened again, I am glad to say.

We did have one small theft that gave us quite a lot of amusement. In a very mixed lot of objects we had cleared from a cottage were two horrid little china dogs, cheap and modern, and ridiculously marked by some hopeful foreign maker with the Chelsea gold anchor. A stallholder we had never trusted, and who was always bragging about his clever buys, came in. He was a man I rarely turned my back on if there was anything small and tempting standing about. This time I did for a moment, and I saw the empty place on the shelf almost before his car shot down the village street.

"Blimey, Chelsea," I could hear him muttering. He came back some months later, for he was the irrepressible type of petty pilferer who I really think did not see any harm in pocketing the odd trifle. He was as garrulous as ever, but this time I did not turn my back, nor could I resist saying, "Didn't you have a pair of little dogs some time ago with gold anchor marks on them? Did you do well with them?" His attractive brown eyes swivelled a little in his head for a moment. "Can't remember," he said and picked up a vase that was a lot more expensive than the things he usually bought. "Think I'll take this," he remarked, and then had the effrontery to add, "Can you make it a trade price?" "No," I said, "I'm afraid I can't this time." "Well, no harm in asking," he remarked airily. I didn't see him again, and I've sometimes wondered if he's "inside". Yet in a way I've missed him, for he was a good natured rogue, full of tall stories and entertaining Cockney boasting.

And all this time I was learning not only about people, but about antiques in general. I had got past the stage of being the little junk shop near the church, patronised by the village. It was time to have notepaper printed, and cards too. I had to decide on a name for the shop. "Just Antiques" seemed too grand and important, for a great deal of my stock was still of the odds and ends type of stuff. Yet "The Junk Shop" sounded a little too disparaging.

I remembered a friend of mine of years ago who had called her shop "The Quaint Conceit", only to discover to her alarmed concern that she was quoting from Samuel Pepys, who had written "Last night I pleasured the scullery maid on the kitchen table. She with her boots on, a quaint conceit."

In the end, after a lot of thought, the only name for my shop that seemed both factual and sensible, turned out to be "Antiques and Things", which it has always remained.

The disgruntled can remark disagreeably, "'Things' is certainly right," and the kinder "But what an enticing description, one never knows what one will find."

The Showroom

As the business grew a plan was developing in my mind. I had decided that if we could spare the space we would turn our dining room into another showroom holding a better type of stock, more carefully displayed, than the jumble of oddments we showed in the little lock-up shop and the barn. It was an attractive room, with an open fireplace and oak beams and a Georgian window. We had the walls distempered white, and then hunted about for a hardwearing but good carpet that would cover the floor. I was lucky enough to find a very heavy Turkish one in soft blue and deep, tawny orange for £20. It has been in constant use now for over ten years, and when it was cleaned about two years ago it looked as good as ever. We had four wall lights fitted, and one spot light that could be trained on to any object that we were particularly proud of and wanted to show off.

I can still remember the stock that room contained when we first opened it. There was a very large but beautifully coloured early Victorian sideboard. On one end stood an oil lamp with a crimson glass bowl, then a collection of Staffordshire animals and two Leeds strawberry dishes. In the centre of the room was a large rosewood table and four cabriole legged chairs with moss green velvet seats. A whatnot crowded with small pieces of china, silver and bronze, and four or five very fine rummers stood near the fireplace, and a magnificent rocking horse filled up the window.

How I wish I had that roomful of stock now! I don't think anything was priced higher than £20, but it all looked charming, and before very long everything was sold. Over the years, as stock became harder and harder to acquire, I did my best to make that showroom look lived in, and put things in juxtaposition so that they enhanced each other, giving people an idea how they could look in their own homes.

I think quite a number of people don't realise that the actual bodily strain of being a dealer can be very heavy. I have been accused of rupturing two of my male helpers over the years by buying too heavy pieces of furniture just because they seemed a bargain, and heaven knows the times I have been bent double myself with a strained back, and had pulled muscles in my arms.

Inevitably someone arrives at the end of a long day to pick up a large chest of drawers. Inevitably, too, after a struggle in the stifling heat or the bitterly cold east wind, it is discovered that the chest will not fit in the van, but has to be heaved up on to the roof rack. You cannot even curse the man who is collecting for being so late, for he turns out to be a friend of the purchaser who is doing a favour he now bitterly regrets. You struggle on, and meanwhile the saucepan on the stove burns dry, and the dogs pad about dismally, wondering if they will ever get their supper.

But this, I suppose, must be counted as an occupational hazard, there are snags in every job. But in mine at least there is also an immense amount of pleasure and excitement, which is more than can be said for most.

A Call Out

One of the most exciting events for a dealer is to have a sudden "call out". This means that a private individual comes into your shop, or phones you to say they have a number of things for sale. They are moving into a smaller house, or are emigrating, or else some aged relation has died, leaving them to dispose of a whole house or cottage full of unwanted stuff. However many times one has been disappointed, and arrived to find only a lot of worthless rubbish, with all the best pieces weeded out by friends and relatives before one arrives, hope always springs eternal in the dealer's breast. This time, we imagine, there will be priceless china, lovely old chests, and tables hidden beneath layers of dirt – and the sellers are only longing to be rid of things; they even state a price that is very reasonable, but not so low that we feel in honour bound to offer more. Of course, in reality it never happens quite like that, although there have been times when a "call out" has proved very lucrative.

I can remember one occasion when this happened, although at the time we very nearly backed out at the last minute, so daunting did the task appear.

We were given the address of a remote little farmhouse, and told that the late owner had just died in an old people's home, where he had been for six years. Nothing had been touched, but now the house was to be sold and the new owners wanted us to clear the whole place for the builders, who were starting modernisation in a fortnight's time. We had been given a nice old key, asked to look over the place that day, and phone our offer that evening, and if it was accepted get busy as soon as possible.

The outside of the house was charming but utterly neglected, and as the door opened reluctantly on squeaking hinges we involuntarily stepped back a pace. A heavy, mud-coloured curtain swung between the door frames, there was a cloud of dust, and that indescribable smell of dirt and decay, of old, unwashed clothes and rotten vegetables.

"I don't think we can," I said, and peered into the sitting room, dark with cobwebs, the windows obscured by long dead pot plants, the fireplace littered with ashes and rusty kettles, while the big round table was still strewn with dirty plates and opened tins of what had once been food. Yet as I spoke my eyes discovered a small antique bureau, a Georgian side table and some very pretty chairs.

I took a deep breath and opened the flap of the desk. Among the litter of papers and letters I saw a tortoiseshell snuff box, a silver watch and chain, a jumble of old seals and a carved ivory figure. The top drawer, however, was stuffed with old bandages, frayed ties and what appeared to be unwashed socks. Holding our breath, we crossed the room and threw open the larder door. Its shelves were stacked to the ceiling, mostly with empty jam jars and rusting tins, but here and there was an old blue and white or lustre jug. There was a huge Wedgwood cheese dish, while the piles of plates looked hopeful.

The bedrooms yielded a walnut chest of drawers, a card table and an oak mule chest, amongst a welter of hideous, cheap dressing tables, unwholesome looking commodes, feather beds and grey blankets.

By this time we had got all the doors and windows open. Drawers held anything from false teeth to silver boxes, and everywhere there were heaps and bundles of old newspaper cuttings and ancient farming magazines. Two hours later we felt we had really only scratched the surface, but we both knew it was a challenge we could not resist.

I phoned the owners that evening. "About the contents of Apple Tree Farm, Mr B," I started.

"Well?" I heard the slight note of nervousness in his voice.

"The thing is, it's terribly difficult to make an offer. You see, there are so many things to be taken into consideration."

"I know, I know – you're telling me," he groaned, "and it means you won't take it on. I shall just have to burn the lot."

"For heaven's sake don't do that, and that wasn't what I meant at all. It's just I really don't know what *is* a fair price to offer – it's a terribly hard job, but there are things there of real value, and we may find more as we go along."

"Look," Mr B said. "Quite frankly, we don't care what you find. Uncle Simon was a real old bastard. We don't want anything that was his. I know what a hell of a state it's in, but my wife loves the house, and if you can get it clear of all the old man's muck, that's the chief thing. In fact, I'd almost pay you to take it away, but the old devil owed me a bit of cash and it's always rankled, so if I can get that back I'm quite satisfied." And he named a sum that took my breath away, when I considered what was there.

"No, we'll have to pay more than that," I told him, and finally we agreed on a price that I knew was going to give us a handsome profit, combined with hours of exciting but very hard and unpleasant work.

Often in the days that followed I bitterly regretted having taken on such a task. We managed to get a gipsy friend to help us, and he carried off a great deal of scrap iron, feather beds, tin baths, saucepans and enamel pails. He was always cheerful, too, which was a great help, and seemed genuinely pleased when we discovered a long gold chain in an old collar box, and some rare botanical books with hand coloured plates. I think he probably made a few finds on his own account, that disappeared into his pockets, but he was such a tower of strength, both mentally and physically, I did not grudge them to him. I don't know what we should have done without him. He made the most enormous bonfires of the utter rubbish, but there we had to watch him rather carefully, as at one point I found him about to heave some nice old peck measures and three milking stools on to the blaze.

"Whatever do people want wormy old stuff like that for?" he asked. "Why, I've burnt scores of them in the past."

"Well, bring them to us instead, in future."

"I will that," he promised, and as a matter of fact he did, often, in the years that followed.

It took us nearly a week to clear Apple Tree Farm, and each day we arrived home with a van full of goods, but worn out and longing to get into a hot bath. But we had made a few really exciting finds: not anything of exceptional value, but interesting and charming oddments. The bureau turned out to be burr elm under its layers of grime, and was very unusual, containing five secret drawers, unfortunately empty except for one rather pathetic love letter. So I suppose Uncle Simon must have been human once upon a time, and someone had loved him.

But "call outs" like this one are very few and far between. More often one is given a glowing description and goes miles, only to find the goods are mediocre, and that the owners have had every dealer in the county in, and are trying to make them bid one against the other. I have sometimes made an offer, to be told at once, "Oh, Mr So-and-so from Colchester offered . . ." and usually the price you have suggested is doubled. "Fair enough, then you had better accept it," I say.

"Well, now you are here can't you make it something nearer his? 'We'd really rather sell the things to you."

I am afraid these sort of remarks no longer cut any ice with me. Maybe I have grown cynical. In the past I used sometimes to phone up the dealer in Colchester or wherever, to ask why he had made such a large offer. "Was there something that I had missed?" I asked. It often turned out that he had actually made a lower bid for the stuff than I had. "They all try it on, these tough ones, trying to play one of us against another," he told me, "and as a matter of fact I no longer make offers to that type of person. I just say, you name a price that will satisfy you, and if I can see my way to paying it, that's O.K."

And now I try to do the same thing. But of course there are times when the person selling really has no idea what to ask, although in these days they are far fewer, when everyone studies saleroom prices, and articles about antiques are in every magazine. Yet when you come up against a genuine innocent, it is very difficult to know exactly what to do, without cheating either yourself or the seller.

There are so many things that have to be taken into consideration that the general public so often fails to understand. Certain things you know you want to buy, but also realise they are going to be very slow sellers, so that your money is going to be tied up for months, sometimes years. With a bit of foresight, a dealer often knows what in the future may become desirable to the public, but meanwhile he has to store the object, keep it from getting damaged – a harder proposition that you might imagine – and all this has to be taken into consideration when naming a price. Sometimes I suggest that the things should be taken to another dealer after I have stated what I will pay, to see if he offers more. But as I know that this is wasting everyone's time, I try to avoid this solution. The people who really rather tax one are those who say, "I know that you are so honest, I'll take whatever you offer."

"But," I tell them, "I may be cheating you unintentionally. I have never sold exactly this type of stuff before."

Sometimes they just say cheerfully. "Well, it's more than I expected anyhow, so I'm quite satisfied, "and everyone is happy. But at other times I suggest that I will pay a certain amount, but price the article rather high, and if I do get this high price I will give the vendor more. We have, in fact, often done so, sometimes very much to the person's surprise, for I am afraid many of them think it is an unlikely thing to happen.

On the other hand, there are those very suspicious characters who burst into your shop months later, saying accusingly, "I see you are asking £2 for that vase I sold you, and you only gave me £3 for the whole lot of things."

It's useless to explain that you only bought the rest of the things to get the little green vase, and they have all been sold at almost no profit. And even if the vase sells at its marked figure, which it may not, you will have made just thirty shillings profit on the whole transaction, and had to wash all the things into the bargain. That type will never think you are telling the truth.

Yet on the whole the people one deals with are very trusting and helpful, and there is no getting away from the fact that there have been occasions when we have cheated people through sheer lack of knowledge.

There are, I'm afraid, just a few people we take a pleasure in diddling a little. For instance, there is a "runner" we sometimes buy from, and he also buys from us. He is a fierce "beater downer", and on many occasions he has sold me things that have been damaged, by craftily keeping his fingers over the chip or crack. So that when occasionally he has something that he does not realise is of value, we negligently scoop it up, and even demand a trade price.

It May Come In Useful

I have a great admiration for those people in the antique business who possess small and immaculately tidy little shops – one is almost tempted to call them boutiques – for personally I am the sort of dealer who is always in a bit of a muddle, and in the process of trying to catch up with unpacking, labelling and making minor repairs. Replacing a broken handle, recovering a stool, or glueing back a loose piece of veneer all takes time, but is well worth doing. I was about to say "never throw away anything that looks vaguely useful," but of course this advice isn't possible to follow unless you have a store-room or sheds of some sort.

The things I am referring to are the odd pieces of carving, the mahogany or gilt finials from a broken cabinet or bracket, the glass knobs, half sets of chessmen, bits of ormolu from bashed up clocks, pieces of mother of pearl, decanter stoppers, beads, the inner lids of tea caddies – in fact, all the innumerable oddments that come a dealer's way, often by chance. But unless you have space to put them out on shelves where they can be seen at a glance, they are apt to waste more time than they are worth. Hidden deep in drawers, stored away in boxes, they can become something of a nightmare.

You *know* you have four red silk tassels that will just finish off the little gilt stool to perfection, but where on earth did you put them so carefully? The hunt goes on, the floor becomes strewn with paper. You discover to your fury a carved gilt rose that would have been the perfect finish to the damaged mirror you sold so cheaply a week before; two ivory caddy handles that you had forgotten you possessed, but never a sign of the red silk tassels and cord. They, no doubt, will turn up long after the stool has been sold. So, as I have discovered the hard way, the only thing to do is to fit a shed or a boxroom up with open shelves, where everything is in full view. Don't bother about the dust – that can soon be got rid of when the time comes to use the object. But I would give one hearfelt warning – never, but never, allow another dealer loose in this storeroom. He will inevitably pounce on something with cries of delight, "This is just what I need to finish off that workbox, that decanter set, that bracket! How much do you want for it?" and he waves the object at you. It is probably worth almost nothing, so you weak-mindedly say he can have it – after all, you have kept it for six months and found no use for it. But mark my words, next week it is the very thing that would have turned a piece of junk into something highly desirable and very saleable. So if you are wise you will keep that storeroom locked, and visit it by stealth when no one is likely to follow you.

We know two nice but wicked old men who are the world's worst bodgers. They have attended sales for years, and gradually filled their spare rooms with all the broken and dilapidated junk that the average dealer cannot face. Then, at the long kitchen table in the evenings they sit chuckling and working away with their pots of glue and plaster, their pieces of wire and bent pins, gold paint from Woolworths, strips of old velvet, and piles of ancient newspapers to stick on the backs of frames or old boxes, preferably with an ancient date in evidence. I have even known them replace missing pieces of pottery and china with carefully chewed chewing gum, painted over with poster paints and finished with a dab of nail varnish. They are proud and delighted with the results, and quite convinced that no one will discover what they have done. Perhaps some unfortunates really don't, but when we bought from them, as we sometimes did, for over the years they had collected some weird and charming objects, we would have to spend long hours unpicking and unsticking, and sometimes even boiling apart their handiwork. Yet most of their labour is spent on gaudy oddments that neither warrant it nor will bring them much return, even if they do sell, so I have come to the conclusion that they really do believe that their work must be Art for Art's sake.

The Right Way to Repair

If you acquire some dilapidated but beautiful piece of furniture or china it is well worth while keeping it until you can persuade an expert to deal with it, even if this means waiting months. And I can assure you it is likely to, for repairing experts are like gold and not to be found easily, or treated lightly when found. Stick to him, should you discover one, like a leech, and never try to hurry him or dare to grumble at delays. I sometimes think if I had my life over again I would take up china repairing, for I feel sure there is a great deal of money to be made in this field. But I doubt, really, if I should have the patience, for it is niggling, finicky work, and I am inclined to be in far too much of a hurry to see results. That is why, in the past, I used to try one cabinet maker after another, because I had heard they were quick. They often were, with disastrous results.

However, my present partner, who is of a much less impatient nature, has taught himself to repair china, so long as the damage is not too great. He started on Staffordshire figures and Victorian vases that were not very valuable, but has now progressed to quite complicated pieces that have had to have whole parts made up.

He works with a mixture of epoxy resin and titanium dioxide, which forms a hard material looking like fine white china, even though it can be sanded into shape. In small sections it has the characteristic "ring" of china, and so helps to preserve the true nature of the repaired piece. It has two drawbacks, though – it is very slow to set, and so needs careful support to avoid sagging; and once set it is so strong and adheres so well, that it is very difficult to correct mistakes. Often a piece of lovely china comes into the shop which has been repaired clumsily with one of the epoxy-type adhesives, and much time is lost taking it to pieces again.

May I ask any keen beginner who wants to repair something really good, to use an old fashioned glue or a rubber-based adhesive, so that one day an expert can deal with it more easily? By all means stick back into place every little broken piece – at least they will not then be lost for ever. But please don't stick them so that their subsequent removal may endanger the whole thing. One day, after much practice, you will realise that your skill has greatly improved, and then you will be ready to make a correction yourself, this time in a strong and permanent form.

When you do get to this stage you will find that a box full of sand will help you to wedge china that is being repaired in such a position that the joined bits will not slip apart. Plasticine and sellotape can also be used to keep small pieces together while the resin sets, usually a matter of two or three days. It will harden more quickly if it can be placed over a radiator or on a hot water tank. Any adhesive that has pushed out of the join can sometimes be removed very carefully with a sharp knife before it has completely hardened, but usually it is better to sand it after it has become completely hard, using a very fine grade glass paper, or possibly a manicure emery board.

It is often a difficult job to match colours and copy small portions of a design. Usually, the more complicated the pattern the easier it is to approximate both to the colour and design; but in all cases where we have made a repair, we state the fact clearly on the price ticket. Private customers often don't mind at all, and are glad to get a good piece at a moderate price.

I personally would infinitely prefer a really beautiful bit of damaged china to a more mediocre piece that was whole. Often the really rare examples do have some damage, which is very understandable, when you consider how they have survived at all over the years, so that it seems unreasonable to expect to find a great many completely unscathed specimens.

In my own home I have a great many pieces that are damaged, and people very rarely notice the fact – not that I mind if they do. Once a dealer friend, looking at a large blue and white Delft vase on my corner cupboard exclaimed enviously, "I wish I could afford to keep a thing like that. It must be worth nearly £100."

I got it down, blew off the dust, and stood it on the table. It is in eleven pieces, and both handles have been stuck on. I bought it for thirty bob from a rag and bone man, who was going to sling it on a dump. Even with all its damage, specialists in Delft have often tried to buy it, but it's not for sale. It gives me a great deal of pleasure, and at the buying price I feel I am not being unduly extravagant in keeping it.

I am sure, too, that one learns far more, both in understanding values and appreciating beautiful things, even if one can only afford to put damaged pieces into one's home and place them among the other treasures, where the eye constantly dwells on them, often quite unconsciously.

"You must get your eyes to really *see*" were the words of one of my teachers when I was a student.

It is, in fact, surprising how long it can take to have a "seeing eye". I suppose we all remember when, as children, the scales seemed to fall from our eyes quite suddenly, and we beheld things as it were for the first time. Much the same thing happens to you when you become an antique dealer. You are confronted with a room full of rubbishy furniture and bric-a-brac, but one or two things will stand out as the only bits worth looking at in the whole place. A table, a print, a tiny pair of old scales, and a Worcester saucer, on a table top massed with plastic spoons and cheap metal pepper pots, stained tea cosies and plaster Bambis – you know then that you have acquired a "seeing eye".

The "Knocker Boys"

It is, I suppose, the constant sense of change and adventure that keeps us going, for there is no getting away from the fact that the junk and small antique dealer is up against a very cut-throat business these days. Gone is the time when people gladly sold you their old things when they grew tired of them, and often expressed pleasure at getting more than they had expected.

One of the real menaces in this trade are those people known as the "knocker boys". They go from house to house, leaving no district untouched. They usually begin by asking if the inmates have any old clocks that won't go, that they would like to sell. Now, nearly every cottage and household has one or two of these – too good to throw away, maybe, yet the cost of repair is excessive. The knocker is asked in. Once he is in it won't be only rubbishy old clocks he goes away with, you can be sure.

Their way of business is much the same as it has always been. A largeish sum is offered for something that the householder has probably bought only a few years ago, and the price of which he may very well remember, so that he accepts the offer with pleasure, convinced that he has discovered a very generous, or very stupid buyer. Then, rather casually, the knocker gets round to the things he really has his eye on. "That old table has had a lot of hard wear," he says. "But I'd take it off your hands, and I'd give you a bob or two for those vases – save your wife a deal of fiddly dusting." So it goes on, and soon the knocker has been through every room in the house. He may not succeed in getting all he wants this first time, but if there is something really worth while it's ten to one he'll tip off a friend, who will soon arrive with a seemingly much better offer, although probably well below the article's real value. If the knocker's victims are old, it is likely they can be frightened or coaxed into making a deal. The conversation goes something like this:

"You can't want that great big old desk, Ma – it's taking up half the room."

"I know, but that's always been promised to my grandson, Terry."

"I'd bet you a pound he'll never use it – he wants up to date stuff. Now how's his place furnished? Tell me that, Ma."

"Well, he has got a lovely three piece suite . . ."

"There you are! What's this shabby old desk going to look like alongside of that?"

The talk may last for quite a while. The knocker also suggests why shouldn't the cottager enjoy the money herself? "Think what a lot that grandson is earning, compared to what you did."

And so it goes on, and the few worthwhile pieces of furniture disappear from the cottage, and when the doctor or some friend from the village next calls, and sees the empty space and hears the price received, they haven't the heart to say, "Oh, but I would have gladly given you five times that amount, only I didn't want to take the one good thing you possessed from you and your children."

Nor are the knocker boys abashed by large houses and well educated owners. Their patter changes and they suggest that probably in a large house of this sort there must be a number of things not used, or else put away in boxes, because of shortage of staff. This is generally true, and sometimes it seems a heaven-sent opportunity to get rid of some of the junk that is constantly being pushed from spare room to attic and from attic to stable. Also, these people, who have inherited a great many of their possessions, may have very little idea of their present-day value, and once again the buyer makes a good killing. The hateful thing is that these men boast of their clever cheating. I remember one particularly nasty story of how they arrived at a small farmhouse to find its owner drunk, and bitterly worried about the funeral expenses for his wife, who had died only two days before. He was listened to with a great show of sympathy, and then was asked if by any chance he possessed anything made of gold, such as old bracelets or brooches belonging to his wife. It would, it was argued, be much better to give her a really grand funeral than have bits and pieces of hers lying about, reminding the old farmer of happier days.

Their two hours' time was well spent. For just over £30 they acquired nearly £400 worth of gold trinkets, and three beautiful antique silver watches. Their boasting in the pub that night knew no bounds.

So rather sadly one sometimes ceases to wonder why antique dealers are held in mistrust by certain sections of the public. Yet, of course, all dealers must depend to a certain extent on "runners" or "knockers" who bring their goods to the door. After a while you can generally judge who are the fairly honest ones, and refuse to buy from the ones you know to be unscrupulous. You have to take the rest on trust – it's a rather "I'm all right, Jack" attitude, I expect. In other words, if their price to you is one that will give you a reasonable profit, buy, and don't ask questions. After all, they may not have cheated anyone – and if they have, you try to tell yourself, possibly the person deserved to be cheated, and there are occasions when one is inclined really to believe this is the case.

On many occasions we have visited a cottage where someone is moving and wishes to sell a few things, to be told, "I have got rid of quite a lot of stuff to a man who called at the door. He seemed ever so glad to take it, and I thought it would get some of it out of the way."

You pick up a cracked Spode plate, and are told, "Oh, there was a whole set of that which he took, but he left the broken bits behind." What can you say to someone in so much of a hurry they could not even wait to show what they had to sell to the dealer they had asked to call – on a day, mark you, fixed by them. Sour grapes, perhaps, but I rather think that lady deserved to be cheated, as I discovered later she certainly had been.

There are, of course, many very reputable "runners" who travel miles, scouring the countryside for things that can be bought easily and cheaply in one district, to bring them to shops eagerly awaiting them many hundreds of miles away. They pay the prices asked without quibbling, they often buy from you as well as selling to you, and the worst crime I think they can be accused of, is avoiding paying quite as much Income Tax as the rest of us. But who's to prove even that?

At any rate, if it wasn't for them our stock would be less interesting and varied, and these regular callers soon get to know what you are looking for, and what prices you will be prepared to pay.

Collectors

Many people come into an antique dealer's with requests for some specific thing.

"We have decided to start a collection of button hooks" or whatever their fancy has strayed to in a moment of sudden enthusiasm. Or sometimes they come for advice, asking one what would be a "good" thing to start making a collection of. This is a pretty difficult thing to give advice on. One is, of course, tempted to say, "Why not start on salt cellars or card cases?" knowing that you have a large number of these particular items in stock that you are anxious to sell. But this is really rather unfair, and the best thing to do is to get your would-be collectors to have a slow look round your showroom and find something that really appeals to them, and start from there. It is quite extraordinary the things that can and do make very interesting collections, and where two or three similar objects in a home might be of little value, the same kind of things in a large quantity, each varying slightly in design, colour or material, can be extremely fascinating.

There is, too, for this type of customer, all the excitement of the chase. He has the legitimate excuse of going from shop to shop in pursuit of his chosen objects. He can, of course, at times be a bit of a bore to the dealer, when he insists on describing in detail all the finds and treasures he has already come across on his travels. But not often; most shopkeepers have great sympathy for this type of customer, for as likely as not the dealer too is an avid collector of something himself.

It is quite amazing what curious objects people will become interested in, and what a variety there is to be found, once you really get dug into your pursuit. Snuff boxes, card cases, stamp holders, button hooks, coffee cans, old biscuit tins, soap dishes, can all make charming and worthwhile collections that grow in value as they grow in interest.

I can remember a small boy who years ago started to acquire any little china boxes with lids that I had in the shop. In those days they often cost only a few pence, and included Goss trinket boxes, small round decorated rouge and powder pots, lettered fish and pomade ones, and the charming little sugar bowls from children's tea sets. As time went on and his pocket money increased, he became more ambitious, and he would pounce on the gold and red glass boxes, or an agate one with a little crack, maybe, that I let him have cheaply, and on one occasion, with his reluctant mother's help, he bought a lovely Leeds mustard pot.

I knew it was not only to my shop that he came, although his rounds were rather limited by the facts that he came on his bicycle or with his mother on her visits to the village stores for groceries. The time came when I did not see him often, as he had gone away to an agricultural training school in Somerset. His mother still came in occasionally, and I always enquired about him.

"Peter is very keen to join some other youngsters and go on a trip in a minibus across Europe this summer," she told me, "but I don't think we shall be able to afford it."

"He had better sell his collection," I suggested.

"I think he would even do that, but he's never paid more than a few shillings for anything, so I don't expect it would help much."

Yet a month or two later his mother phoned me to say he had done just that. "And you'll never believe this possible," she burbled, "but he made over a hundred pounds with all that old junk that I often tried to stop him buying. He says he's going to start another collection as soon as he gets home again."

Well, I wish him luck, but I am afraid that he won't find it quite as easy as he did in the past.

Yet there are still things to be found cheaply, if you have the patience and study your subject well. Fans and dolls may have gone way out beyond the reach of most of us, but there are still interesting old wooden kitchen implements, carpenter's tools, brass animals, finger bowls, unusual pepper pots, medals and plaques given as prizes, books on cookery, ash trays and pickle forks. My advice is, buy something a little unusual, small and at the time of buying not very expensive, and which has a definite appeal for you, and go on from there. You will be amazed how soon you will find "your thing" lurking in the most unlikely places, at jumble sales and on market stalls, or despised and unwanted in a friend's house; and how soon, too, you will go like a water diviner straight to your chosen object, as it lies disregarded under a heap of rubbish.

But there seems no end to the things that are collector's items to some people. I once had a man in my shop who told me in all seriousness that he went in for fire engines and old fire fighting equipment. I happened to know of an old, horse-drawn fire engine mouldering away in a farm shed. I gave him the address but I never heard any more, so I am rather afraid he was too late, and someone else had got there first.

I can also recall one charming, rather vague looking man who often wandered into my shop on Sunday mornings. I was not supposed to be open on that day, but I was often working there, and the door would be ajar. He would quietly potter about, not speaking much, until one day I asked him if he was looking for anything specially – did he collect? He gave me a sudden wide smile that completely changed his rather withdrawn expression. "Yes," he said, "I collect pornographic things, but only pretty ones, and they are quite difficult to find these days."

I was once brought a cigar case by a very old lady, who unwrapped it rather furtively, with many glances over her shoulder, lest anyone else come into the shop. "I would like to sell this. It was my father's – he was, well, rather a racy type of man, but he always said that this was a very good painting. Although," she went on in a rush, "I don't think *good* is quite the word. Maybe realistic or clever is nearer the mark."

Actually, it was a charming painting of a voluptuous nude woman, rather in the manner of Etty, but more lively. The old lady was delighted with the price I paid, and I sold it within three days.

Saucy Victorian postcards also sell well, and I am afraid we have sometimes been guilty of selling a rather dull postcard album, by the trick of inserting one or two slightly risque nudes or questionable joke postcards, and it is surprising how very rude seaside cards can be if you come to study them, and have still got by the censor of the twenties and thirties.

Village Sales

I suppose all country antique dealers look back with nostalgia to the days when sales were most frequently held in marquees in the grounds of the house of the owners of the goods for sale. The viewing day was often in the house, with the furniture in its original position, and glass, china and silver placed in the centre of the larger rooms on tables and trestles. In the huge old kitchens all the cooking utensils and crockery were laid out, while in the stables was a great miscellany of garden implements of all kinds – harness and bath chairs, perambulators and dog baskets.

It was very pleasant to wander over the big house, lose one's way in the passages and attics, and wonder in amazement at the army of servants it must have taken to run the place in its heyday.

Often these great houses still only boasted two bathrooms to a dozen bedrooms or more – one often with a fireplace, a great mahogany edged bath and a basin supported on wonderful cast iron brackets, while the second, if there was one, was in the servants' quarters – a narrow iron tub on strange iron paw feet and a small wash basin was probably all it held, the floor still covered in brown linoleum and a roller blind at the window.

For the day of the sale everything would be brought out into the big marquee by the porters, and held up in front of the auctioneer's rostrum to be viewed by the mass of people sitting in the chairs or huddled in groups about the entrance to the tent, their catalogues in their hands, their eyes alert, their pencils poised to write down the price of each lot.

I seem to remember those days as always being hot and sunny, with the smell of the trampled grass beneath one's feet, the patter and jokes of the auctioneer, and an air of expectancy hanging over everyone, even the hard-boiled members of the Ring. Apart from the many dealers there was always a big gathering of semi-county ladies who seemed to frequent all the sales in the countryside, although quite often they did not buy a thing. They arrived early, with picnic hampers, dogs, children, flasks of coffee or whisky, and generally appropriated the front seats. Occasionally their chatter would disturb the auctioneer and he would call out plaintively, "Ladies, ladies, there is going to be a break for lunch at one o'clock – save it up till then, if you please."

And indeed that lunch hour, sitting in the grounds of the old and often beautiful houses, held an enchantment touched, sometimes, with sadness as to the fate of the old place, that seldom enters into the sales one attends today.

I can remember another sale at a large old farmhouse, where everything was sold on the lawn at the edge of the moat. It was a charming setting, although wild and untidy, for the place had been neglected for years. Everything was to come under the hammer, and I can well imagine that the auctioneers must have had an almost impossible job sorting the things into any kind of order.

Apart from the usual run of furniture and household oddments, there were Edwardian dresses in heavy satins and lace, madly over-trimmed and enormous hats, sporty blazers and men's boaters, kid shoes and lace fichus. It was August, and there were a number of young people there who could not resist this kind of gear, although it was long before such things had become the rage. They bought them for a few shillings, and before long were disappearing behind bushes, to walk out a few minutes later, clad in their purchases. It turned into a day of craziness – dogs and children rushing hither and thither, one child falling in the moat and climbing out covered with duck weed and mud, to the applause of the crowd and wails of despair from a harassed mother.

That was the day, too, on which I found a set of hand-coloured prints of Leach pictures on the rubbish heap – rather surprisingly, in the circumstances. I had the honesty to report my find to the harassed auctioneer. "Oh, give me a bob," he shouted, which I very quickly did, and stowed them away in the boot of the car before he thought again. Framed, they brought me quite a lot of money, for there were twenty-four of them.

They were good fun, those sales, but my goodness they were often terribly exhausting as well. For at the end of a blazing summer afternoon, to pack up box after box of heavy china and pots, gather together all the odd bits of bric-a-brac and furniture that you had been unable to resist buying because they had gone so cheaply, and then stagger, clutching these objects, to the car, which might have had to be parked quite a long way away, needed a great deal of physical effort. Sometimes one of those hangers-on who always seem to frequent sales could be persuaded to help for the price of a drink or two, but in those days I hadn't much extra cash to spare that would have also left my purchases as bargains. So usually the friend who had taken me to the sale and I struggled backwards and forwards with our burdens over the rutted grass, thinking longingly of the cup of tea or a strong drink the moment we got home.

Of course, really, there were sales held in marquees on bitterly cold days, which one struggled to attend with the often mistaken idea that the howling east wind would keep other people away, and one would come home with the bargain of the year. Generally, all the other dealers seemed to have had the same thought, and I think I got more bargains in the hot summer days, when people were inclined to wander away to get a cold drink, and the whole atmosphere was less tense. In the bitter cold one was inclined to feel "Well, hell's bells, I will take home as much as I can, after coming all this way and suffering this rotten wind."

But nowadays these sales are few and far between, and nearly everything is sold in the salerooms of the nearest big town.

My Helpers, and Dealers Who Specialise

Over the years my business was growing, sometimes with almost alarming rapidity. It meant that I had to try to find replacements for my stock each week, and have a spare shed full of priced and labelled articles ready to go into the showroom or the little shop, at a moment's notice. Owing to ill health my husband was forced to retire some time before we had planned. He could, of course, help me a great deal with the paperwork, but he did not like buying or pricing things, nor could he carry heavy furniture or boxes. As the little shop with the bow window was about fifty yards up the road from he showroom in the house, and the furniture store in the barn, it did mean a great deal of running about for me, and there were still meals to be cooked and a certain amount of housework to be done – although I tended to skimp that rather. So in the end we decided we must have some help, but the trouble was that we could not afford to pay out much in wages.

It was then that Mrs Gowing came to our rescue. She was the widow of the village baker, and in the old days had run his shop, selling cakes and sweets while her husband did the baking and the bread round.

"I miss my little shop so much," she said, "I wondered if you would let me sit in yours and take care of it in the afternoon? I wouldn't want any pay, it's just that I like things going on, and as it's just opposite my cottage I can keep an eye on that too."

It turned out to be a first-rate idea. Mrs Gowing, although nearly eighty, was a splendid sales lady. She recorded each item sold in a long account book, and although her descriptions of them tended to puzzle me at times, I knew that the afternoon's takings would all be scrupulously noted down. I had persuaded her to take a commission of two shillings in the pound, although there were occasions when she flatly refused to do so. "Why, it didn't take me five minutes to sell that – it just sold itself."

In vain did I point out to her that there were afternoons when she might sit for two hours or more, and not take any commission at all.

"No, I can't take it, I haven't earned it." And there the matter ended, and I must say there were times when I was very grateful, for things were not always easy, because I was putting what I now realise was far too small a margin of profit on my goods.

After a few months another old age pensioner who lived in the almshouses, suggested she would like to "sit in" on Saturday mornings, when Mrs Gowing could not come. Naturally I consulted Mrs Gowing about this, for I did not want her to think she was being ousted in any way, to discover that it was she who had put the idea into Mrs Fowler's head. They were a wonderful pair, and Mrs F worked for me until a few months before her death, while Mrs Gowing did give up rather reluctantly after her ninetieth birthday. She still takes a great interest in the business, and often some of our old customers pop over to her cottage to have a little natter with her.

She still lives alone, cooks her own meals, and in winter there is always a bright fire burning and her room looks charming with its pots of flowers, Staffordshire figures and oil paintings of horses, that came from the sale at "the big house" forty-five years ago, but which I think she has learned to treasure and see with a new eye since she worked in an antique shop.

Soon after this, a carpenter who lived on the council estate on the other side of the village started to work for us in the evenings and at weekends. He was absolutely indispensable over moving heavy pieces of furniture, replacing missing legs of chests of drawers, and patching oak furniture, although he did not like anything that needed re-veneering.

"I'm not a cabinet maker," he would tell me firmly, and even when I had troubled to find an old and matching piece of veneer off some broken drawer, he would insist it was not possible to use it.

"I'll have to plane it down, and then it's just the same as a new bit."

"Rub down the back, then you will keep the old patina," I would beg. But it was no use – I could talk till I was black in the face, Mr B didn't hold with patina.

"What is it but just a lot of old dirt and grease?" he would say.

But many were the jobs, if they were straightforward and took his fancy, he would do beautifully, and his willingness to move furniture and load up customers' cars was an enormous help to me.

He had a great love of searching for hidden treasure and finding secret drawers in bureaux. He hunted assiduously down the back and arms of sofas and chairs, and was sometimes rewarded by pennies and florins, fountain pens, silver pencils and other oddments, all of which he brought to me in triumph, for he was the soul of honour where I was concerned.

I had turned out an old stable in the garden to be his workshop, for he had explained that at home it was difficult to do much, as his wife insisted that he cleared up each evening when he had finished for the night. This struck me as rather unreasonable of her when I first heard it. But oh! my goodness, didn't I understand her point of view after Mr B had worked for us for a few months. He was for ever finding oddments that had been discarded on the building site that would come in at some time – pieces of moulding, the remains of a tin of stain, some nails and endless offcuts of wood, all of which were brought to the stable each night on his way home from work. He was probably tired and wanting his tea, so everything was flung down wherever there happened to be a space. As the months went by there wasn't a space, but the things still came.

This collecting of useful odds and ends was for our benefit as well as his, of that I am sure, and sometimes he appeared with quite exciting finds in the way of old locks and hinges.

In his first enthusiasm he had put up shelves and made racks for his tools, but after about two weeks with us I don't think I ever saw a tool in its right niche, or a paint pot on the shelf that was supposed to be its proper place. The window, even, became obscured as things of all sorts piled themselves on the sill, and it was soon impossible to close the door. Heaven knows I am not a tidy person myself, but I certainly began to see his wife's point of view.

Every two or three months he would have a turn-out of sorts, and the dustbin would be loaded down with heaps of dirty polishing rags, half used sand paper, shavings and dried up tins of stain or paint from which the lids had been left off. It drove me into a frenzy; but he was so disarmingly kind and cheerful, so what could I say? I did explode into fury on occasions, and we would have a right royal row, for we both had quick tempers. He could not or would not see the time he wasted in trying to find something that should have been ready to his hand. We parted several times, only to make up our differences again, for I think we were very fond of each other, in spite of everything. He could not change, and at last I realised it and tried to have a blind eye, but I often fumed inwardly, and sometimes outwardly too.

On Saturday afternoons we always seemed to have a sort of tea party in the office, where there was a big window that overlooked the garden and the entrance to the furniture showroom. A few moments after I had called Mr B in from his work bench, and settled down with our cups of tea and slices of cake, John and his friend Pat would appear, delivering a dresser or something. I would go to the kitchen and fetch two extra mugs, and before I could pour out who should I see but George, who had brought me some china to look at.

He is a big, burly person who always seems hungry, so I set to to make another pot of tea and find a tin of biscuits or some scones. Mr B settled himself more comfortably into what was known as *his* armchair, scooping the two little dogs on to his lap, out of the way of all the large feet, and we all settled down to another half hour's break.

"I think on Saturday afternoons this should be known as Prynne's Cafe, not the antique shop," a woman friend remarked when she too happened to drop in on one of these Saturday afternoon sessions.

There was, of course, a lot of trade gossip and stories of how well other dealers were doing, but there was also some business done, and on cold winter afternoons it was a cosy, relaxing half hour in a hard-working, often frustrating week.

All of these strong young men have helped me a great many times in emergencies, and if sometimes now I find their casual habit of wandering in and making themselves tea in my very small kitchen, rather exasperating, I try to remember this, and not get irritated and snappy in my old age. I am really very lucky that they still remain my friends after so many years.

I depended a lot, during my husband's illness, on the help of a woman friend who had a good deal of time on her hands, as her children were both at school and she had recently divorced her husband. She was very interested in antiques and was quite willing, if I paid the petrol, to take me out in her car on buying trips. We scoured the district, answering advertisements and visiting other junk shops and sale yards. We both enjoyed it enormously, for even if we did not buy much, we both loved Suffolk and Norfolk countryside. We took by-roads whenever it was possible, and in that way we often came upon an unexpected small shop where we might find treasures. Also, we discovered lovely, unspoilt places to picnic in the summer, while in the winter we found many an excellent lorry drivers' pull-up, where we enjoyed succulent bacon and eggs with chips.

There was also a woman dealer friend I went out with on this sort of trip, on occasion. She was a small person but she drove a super, ancient Rolls Royce. You could hardly see her behind the driving wheel, and I suppose she really ought not to have driven such a car at all. She had an amazing capacity for crowding our various purchases into the back of the car or into the boot, which was invariably tied down with a piece of rope, because it could not be shut, so full was it with our boxes of china and glass. It was often with cheers of amusement, not untinged with derision, that we were greeted in the forecourts of the car-men's pull-ups when we arrived, but we were not deterred, for we knew from experience that those were the places we were likely to get a good meal, whatever the time of day.

Those outings were often good fun. They were hard work too, and sometimes looking back on it I wonder how I got through all I did.

"You're a pig for work," an old man once told me, with a mixture of admiration and irritability, and looking back now I think perhaps he was right, and I neglected things that I should not have done. At any rate I have learned at last not to drive myself quite so hard, but whether from dawning good sense or necessity, I am not altogether sure. I certainly realise that without all my very kind friends I should often have landed myself in the most terrible messes, and to my dying day I shall be grateful to them for all the help they have given me so faithfully over the years.

Taxes

But there was one field of work where outside people could not help me very much, and in which I was particularly hopeless, and my husband, a commercial artist, was little better, and that was in coping with Income Tax returns. Before he retired his agent had dealt with such matters for him, and everything was cut and dried. I soon discovered from talking to other dealers that I was probably not claiming for various items that could be charged up to the business. So on a friend's recommendation we decided to go to an accountant.

That poor man! How he must have suffered, both from my stupidity and the peculiar way I kept my books. An entry in my day book such as "Chest of Drawers – oak – £20 less £3 owing on toy cart," was quite clear to me, at any rate for a few months after I made the entry, but it certainly wasn't to the accountant, nor indeed, if the truth were told, was it to me when he queried it over nine months later. I really struggled very hard to answer his questions, and he did, I am sure, explain things in a way which would have been perfectly understandable to anyone less allergic to figures than I am.

I talked it over with a woman friend who had a stall in the Portobello Road, only to find that she was almost as hopeless as I was myself.

"My accountant said something terrible to me," she told me. "He said, 'Miss R, if you can't fiddle your books more convincingly than this, you had better not try to cheat at all'. And the awful thing was, I was not even thinking of cheating."

It was the same with me. Sometimes I cheated myself, sometimes the tax people, and yet I was completely unconscious of the fact. All the same, I grew to dread the sight of a letter from the accountant. I knew it would be asking endless questions that would take me hours of work to answer, even if I could do so at all. He was very kind and patient with me, considering the bother I must have been to him. I remember once, when I told him I had recommended a friend to go to him. He groaned, "Not someone like you, is it?"

By this time I was beginning to have what seemed to me an enormous turnover that ran into thousands of pounds. This rather alarmed me, although it also filled me with pride when I considered my very modest start. But it puzzled me as well, for we really did not seem all that better off. All our married life my husband and I had had a very precarious income, sometimes doing quite well and living accordingly, I suppose, and sometimes hardly knowing how we were going to pay the grocer's bill.

In the end something always "turned up". My husband got a serial to illustrate, or I sold a story or an article, and the crisis passed. The odd thing was, we never seemed to live very differently either in the hard times or the good. Maybe this has given me this rather haphazard way with cash. It's not that I don't like money and the things and comforts it can buy – I certainly do, for I am a naturally greedy and self-indulgent type of person. But I do also, I think, find a sort of challenge in being hard up and making good use of what little I have got. After all, I do go at least half way with the old song that states that "the best things in life are free".

Nevertheless, although my haphazard approach to money matters gave me months of feeling carefree, the days when I was forced to face reality were correspondingly upsetting. I descended into a depth of worry and despair; I wondered in panic-stricken moments whether I should not give up the business (which I couldn't afford to do anyhow); part with all my stock at cost; take an intelligent, hard-boiled partner; or sell groceries instead.

It was at this time, too, that I was having to give more thought to what I bought. For one thing, I was no longer spending shillings. I was on occasion buying objects that might cost me nearer a hundred pounds than ten. The question was continually arising as to how much one could really afford to pay on an object that was in need of repair.

If it was really beautiful and genuinely antique I found it very hard to resist. "It's only held together by the wood worms holding hands," another dealer told me once, when I showed him a small walnut table I had just bought. My heart sank, and did so still more when I received the restorer's bill. I put that table away and forgot about it, for it worried me whenever I caught sight of it. But a couple of years later I sold it at a handsome profit, wood worm holes and all, so quickly were prices going up. Yet at times one can't afford to have one's money tied up like that, if one is only in a small way of business.

I was now getting almost 50% trade buyers, and although I missed some of the private customers, I had to admit that it was easier selling to "the trade". They knew what they wanted, and they would not bring an object back after a few days because "it didn't quite match the rest of the things in the room."

You had, of course, to give them a trade price, usually about 10% off. It was then that I realised some of my marked prices would not stand that amount of discount. Reluctantly I upped my prices, for there were two of us to keep now, as my husband only had a tiny pension.

It was all growing a little less fun, and gradually, too, a different type of person was opening up in the antiques world. Clever sharp faced young men on the one hand, and the wives of well-off business men on the other.

I can still remember my feeling of irritation one day when a woman who had a weekend cottage in a nearby village came in to tell me she had opened a stall in one of the well-known antique markets in London.

"You see, it's so easy, dear," she burbled. "I just pay the rent of this little stall – I leave it closed when I don't feel like going – but the relief to have somewhere to go to get away from Julian, who really is an old grump now he has retired – honestly, he doesn't take a hairsline of interest in anything, well, not anything interesting, just sits and reads the newspaper all day and glooming over what he reads. Of course, darling, I know how right he is, but what's the use? So I keep one lovely comfy chair behind my little stall, so I can run away from him and sit there. And I meet all sorts of interesting people, and sometimes sell something, and it's all such fun."

"What do you sell?" I asked politely and a little wonderingly.

"Oh, I specialise in snuff boxes. I don't really know anything about them, but if I see a nice one on someone's stall I just buy it and add 25%. And you've no idea how impressive, *really* impressive, about a hundred snuff boxes all on one stall look. People think, 'Gee, she must know her stuff with a collection like that – must be a real specialist – so if I buy from her I'm bound to be O.K.' And they just do – isn't it wonderful?"

"Wonderful," I said, and tried to sound enthusiastic.

Give And Take

You will find that on the whole dealers are quick to send people to friends' shops. "I suppose you get a rake-off," one cynical customer said to me. But this is very rarely the case, although it is sometimes offered when a really large deal comes off through an introduction of this sort.

There is, however, very little of the dog-in-the-manger attitude among the older types of dealer, although there are times when one grinds one's teeth in envy when one hears of someone else pulling off a quick and fat profit by selling something he has just bought from you, and which you have had in your sale room for months at a lower price.

In fact, I did just this thing once myself. A friend with a cottage saleroom had had a very large and handsome sideboard in her place for weeks. It was really too big for the room, and on impulse I acquired it, for I thought it most attractive.

She let me have it very reasonably, and because I found it so useful to show china and plate on, I marked it more than twice the price she had had on it, not half a mile away. I sold it within a week to someone who must have passed it in her showroom a dozen times without seeing it. We both laughed a lot, and very generously she refused to take any more money from me.

Advertising

A great many of my friends in the trade depend on acquiring their stock through advertising in their local papers, and if your shop happens to be tucked away in a side road or in a remote part of the country this is, I think, almost a necessity when you first open. Also, if your shop tends not to look like a shop at all, as many don't, it is quite a good idea to put a few pieces of furniture out on the pavement in front of the place, as you will find these catch the eye of passing motorists more than you would expect.

If, however, you feel this is a rather low-class way of advertising your trade, a well-lettered but large sign is the answer. But do, I beg of you, put out something that is easy to read at a glance. I know one shop owner who was so carried away with the fact that he sold antiques and what are called "bygones" that he had such "olde-worlde" lettering on his signboard it was virtually impossible to read, unless you stopped the car and stood puzzling over it for some while.

After you become really established you will probably find that you need to do very little advertising at all; but by then you will almost certainly find, when you least need it, that a great many persuasive young men will call on you, asking you to insert a half-page advertisement in a recently started trade paper.

We have never done this, but that is not to say that many of my dealer friends have not told me that they do so, with wonderful results. It means, of course, that you must put this cost on to the goods you sell, so that your customers, including even your old regulars who would have come to you anyhow, have to pay that little bit more. Against that you do probably tend to add interesting new collectors who might otherwise never have come to you at all, to your list of buyers. But there is also, I am afraid, a slight risk of crooks getting on to your address in this way, for in these times they are a menace that is certainly on the increase, and it is wise to insure your stock as completely as you can afford, especially if yours is a lock-up shop.

Probably the best advertisement of all is having a stall at one of the well-established Antiques Fairs. It is a splendid way of showing the type of goods you specialise in to an enormous crowd of people, who are reassured by the knowledge that nothing but genuine antiques can be shown, as they all have to pass a committee of experts. Or that at least is the general idea, although at the smaller fairs one does tend to wonder at times quite who those experts were. Still, there is no getting away from the Trades Description rule, and anything in doubt bought at a trade fair can always be taken back, and you can demand that your money is refunded.

If you are young, strong and gregarious, you might do very well by taking a stall at one of the trade fairs in your district. You will meet other dealers, learn a few more tricks of the trade, and may manage to buy quite well for yourself too, for you will get a first look-in before ever the public has a chance. And often what one dealer can sell cheaply for some reason, can be just the thing you have customers lining up for.

Yet when all is said and done I still think the best advertisement is personal recommendation by word of mouth. I can remember feeling very pleased when, once, I asked a new customer where she had heard of my shop, to be told, "Well, as a matter of fact, it was in mid-Atlantic when I was coming home on the Queen Elizabeth, and told a fellow passenger that I was visiting Suffolk, and she said 'Gee, but you must visit the little antique shop where all the American wives from the base go' – and she painted your shop in such glowing terms that I made a note in my diary and here I am."

"I hope you are not disappointed?" I asked, rather apprehensively.

"Not a bit – see what a lot I've bought, and I shall come back with my mother – she can't have discovered you, although she only lives about ten miles from here."

She did too, and I garnered another whole villageful of customers through that chance remark in the middle of the Atlantic.

Something that has made me slightly nervous of putting an illustrated advertisement in a paper, is the feeling that the particular item would have already been sold by the time some of the people came in answer to it. They might have come a long way, and probably arrive when the shop was looking particularly tatty, and would consequently be annoyed and perhaps make understandably unkind remarks, deflating me completely.

You will find that a great many other dealers will recommend you if you are willing to do the same for them; in fact, we often ring each other up if we have a customer in looking for something we can't supply. Admittedly there are a few dog-in-the-manger shop owners who cling on to their richer customers with a fierce tenacity that is almost ludicrous. We have one lady who buys from us occasionally, who always swears us to secrecy about what she has bought.

"You see," she explained nervously, "I live in the same village as Mrs E, and as you know she has a lovely little shop, but she doesn't like me to go anywhere else – she always insists she'll find what I'm looking for in time, but quite often she doesn't. All the same, she would be furious if she knew that I'd been anywhere else, so I have to pretend things have been given to me, if by any chance she comes to the house and sees it."

There is, however, a strict code of fairness about not trying to entice away other dealers' "regulars" by suggesting to them that they are paying more in another shop than they would in yours. Even if you actually know this to be the case, it is unkind and rather unsporting to let down a fellow tradesman. He may have his own particular reason for asking a high price on occasion; it is not for you to judge, but to back him up as far as you can without telling untruths. It is only if you know that an innocent beginner is being victimised by some unscrupulous shopkeeper that you should feel justified in dropping a hint or two to this effect.

Coming back to the subject of advertising, another reason why I tend to shun the direct method is the fact that I am not nearly as sure as most dealers how to describe my goods. I can often judge the age, the quality and the beauty of a certain object without being at all sure of its factory, maker, or even place of origin.

Consequently I am always delighted when I come across well-marked pieces of china and the odd painting with a nicely legible signature. To me personally a signature on a painting means very little except as a thing of commercial value. I have on my walls a number of drawings and paintings that I should hate to part with, but half of them at least have no signature, and those that have I usually forget who they are by, until some friend examines them and reminds me.

It is, however, very exciting to come across some object that really has an authenticated history attached to it. We have had a few things of this sort over the years – old writing boxes initialled and still containing a few letters addressed to the owner, giving details of his or her day to day life. Books with the book plates and signatures of well known people, plates and silver with family crests, and snuff boxes with inscriptions, dates and references to some past event.

Yet perhaps it is nearly as fascinating to think, as you tap an antique barometer dated 1805 that has come from a house in Holt, "Maybe Nelson has done this too, and wondered about the weather to come, just as I am doing at this moment."

Old toys and dolls have a touching air of nostalgia, and some of the most battered and worn seem to convey the message of how intensely they have been loved and quarrelled over in the past, by neat little children in hampering, stuffy clothes. I feel sure the plastic toys, the expensive Chopper bikes and the sophisticated girlie dolls will never receive the same love or long life that the wooden tops, the clockwork trains and games of solitaire and Ludo have. Even I can remember the beautifully illustrated children's books that were only looked at as a special treat on Sunday evening, the pages being carefully turned after you could prove that you had washed your hands.

I used to wonder about the old kitchen utensils that I still use when I am cooking. Were they part of some village bride's first equipment, or had they always remained "below stairs?" I discovered too how much more efficient they are to use than many of the latest gadgets that spin and whirr and chop by electricity, and incidentally take a hell of a time to wash up.

Final Words To Would-be Dealers

A friend, another antique dealer, burst into my office some time ago, looking quite unlike her usual calm and unruffled self.

"Tell me," she asked, "why do so many people seem to think that all antique dealers are a sort of marriage guidance centre?"

We pondered the question for some time and really found no adequate answer. But the fact remains, we do get people pouring out their most intimate problems to us, in a way that I feel sure seldom happens in a grocer's or a dress shop.

Perhaps it is something to do with the more leisurely atmosphere in our business – at least on the surface – or maybe the presence of objects that make people think of their grannies, has this effect on them.

Over the years, all sorts of desperate situations have been expounded to me. Often the only thing one can do is listen with as much sympathy as possible; few people need more than this, but if you are the sort of person who is driven mad by listening to other people's problems it would be best to think twice before entering the antique business.

But above all I think I would say to anyone opening an antique shop "Try to be sympathetic toward your customer's tastes." This can be more difficult than it sounds if you happen to be a person with very definite likes and dislikes. If someone comes in asking for pseudo Dresden shepherdesses or ballerinas, don't shudder and try to sell them a Staffordshire group, which you find irresistible, instead. In all probability they will think your Staffordshire figures both crude and strongly coloured, which they often are, and will completely fail to see their naïve charm. If you do not stock the type of china they ask for, usually spoken of as "figurines" at least try to send them to some place where they are likely to find them.

In the same way you may care passionately for oak and pine furniture, but that is not to say that a room cannot look very charming full of inlaid Edwardian pieces, cut glass vases and imitation horsebrasses.

In the antique trade as in most others always remember that "beauty is in the eye of the beholder" and that maybe you are a bit blind yourself. Give advice when it is asked for, but I beg of you, when you have gained a little specialized knowledge, don't try to cram it down your customers throats because it is always nicer to make your own mistakes in your own way than to be guided ruthlessly on to the path of so-called good taste.